FRONTIER LAND

MOUNTAIN MEN

OF THE FRONTIER

Charles W. Sundling

Visit us at
www.abdopub.com

Published by ABDO Publishing Company, 4940 Viking Drive, Edina, MN 55435. Copyright ©2000 by Abdo Consulting Group, Inc. International copyrights reserved in all countries. No part of this book may be reproduced in any form without written permission from the publisher.

Printed in the United States.

Edited by: Tamara L. Britton
Art Direction: John Hamilton

Cover photo: Corbis-Bettmann
Interior photos: Corbis-Bettmann

Sources: Adams, Alexander B. *Sunlight and Storm: The Great American West.* New York: Putnam and Sons, 1977; *American Heritage History of the Great West, The.* New York: American Heritage, 1965; Encarta 98 Desk Encyclopedia, 1996-97, Microsoft Corporation, 1996; Encyclopedia Britannica, Chicago: Encyclopedia Britannica, Inc., 1993; Gates, Charles M. *Five Fur Traders of the Northwest.* St. Paul: The Minnesota Historical Society Press, 1965; Grolier Multimedia Encyclopedia, The 1995, Grolier Electronic Publishing, 1995; Lamar, Howard (editor). *The Reader's Encyclopedia of the Old West.* New York, 1977; Milner, Clyde A. et. al. (editors). *The Oxford History of the American West.* New York, 1990; Nute, Grace Lee. *The Voyageur's Highway.* St. Paul: The Minnesota Historical Society Press, 1969; Van Every, Dale. *The Final Challenge.* New York: William Morrow, 1964.

Library of Congress Cataloging–in–Publication Data

Sundling, Charles W.
   Mountain men of the frontier / Charles W. Sundling
      p. cm. — (Frontier land)
   Includes index.
   Summary: Discusses some of the explorers and trappers who journeyed west to hunt and trade beaver pelts and other commodities during the early nineteenth century.
   ISBN 1-57765-043-3
   1. Pioneers—West (U.S.)—History—Juvenile literature. 2. Fur traders— West (U.S.)—History—Juvenile literature. 3. Trappers—West (U.S.)—History—Juvenile literature. 4. Frontier and pioneer life—West (U.S.)—Juvenile literature. 5. West (U.S.)—History—Juvenile literature.
[1. Pioneers—West (U.S.) 2. Fur traders—West (U.S.) 3. Trappers—West (U.S.) 4. Frontier and pioneer life—West (U.S.) 5. West (U.S.)—History— To 1848.] I. Title. II. Series: Sundling, Charles W. Frontier land.
F596.S93 2000
978—DC21   98-10144
                                                        CIP
                                                         AC

CONTENTS

A re-creation of the fur trading room at Old Fort William, Thunder Bay, Ontario, Canada. A scale weighs beaver pelts to be bundled and shipped to Europe.

Portrait of two beavers by famed American naturalist and painter John James Audubon.

THE FUR TRADE

A pelt is an animal's skin with its fur or hair still attached. Two hundred years ago beaver pelts were the most desired in the world. Beavers have thick fur that ranges from blonde to black.

Grown beavers are about four feet (1.2 m) long, including their long, flat tails. Beavers weigh about 40 to 60 pounds (18 to 27 kg). They have short legs. They use their front feet, called forepaws, like hands. Their duck-like back feet are big and webbed for swimming.

Beavers use their sharp-edged front teeth to cut trees, which they use to build dams and lodges. The lodges are built in water. Beavers build their lodges with underwater entrances, which block most predators from getting inside.

A beaver dam.

Mountain men and other hunters set traps near beaver lodges to obtain the valuable pelts.

Two hundred years ago most beaver pelts were made into hats. Hat makers cut the long hair from the pelt, revealing the soft underfur.

The underfur was removed from the pelt and made into felt cloth. Then they soaked the cloth in chemicals, which made it long lasting. Pounding it with tools made it easier for hat makers to shape the material.

Hat makers made hats with three corners turned up. These hats were called tricorns. Sometimes they made hats with two corners turned up. They called these bicorns. The hat makers also made stovepipe hats, which looked like the long black pipes that go from a stove to a ceiling.

A man wearing a tricorn hat.

Popular fashion made beaver fur valuable. In Europe and America, men wanted hats made of beaver fur. People who sold beaver pelts to the hat makers made a lot of

John Jacob Astor

money. John Jacob Astor owned a very successful company called the American Fur Company. At the time of Astor's death in 1848, he was worth about $20 million.

William H. Ashley and Andrew Henry began the Rocky Mountain Trading Company. They hired trappers who became famous mountain men. Jim Bridger, James P. Beckwourth, and Edward Rose worked for the Rocky Mountain Trading Company. Jedediah Strong Smith also worked for the company.

Companies had many ways of getting the thousands of beaver pelts they needed. One way was to trade with Native Americans. The companies gave the Native Americans rifles, blankets, and liquor. In return the Native Americans gave beaver pelts.

A second way of getting beaver pelts was to hire trappers. The trappers went west, trapped beavers, and came back with pelts.

Another way was to buy pelts directly from trappers who worked for themselves. These trappers were known as independents. Sometimes they had trapping partners, but most of the time they wanted to trap alone.

A man in nineteenth century trapper costume. Trappers were hired to find beaver pelts to satisfy the demand for beaver hats.

A scout dressed like a mountain man chews on a piece of grass at a Boy Scout Jamboree in Idaho.

ENTERPRISING YOUNG MEN

Good trappers, or mountain men, were enterprising, eager young men. Usually they were loners. They had to be physically strong and able to endure hardship. They also needed intelligence to make quick decisions.

Most mountain men needed two or three horses or mules. They rode one animal and put their supplies on the others. Their supplies included metal traps. The traps were expensive pieces of machinery, each costing close to $15. At this time in history, two tailor-made cotton shirts cost around 60¢. A haircut cost 10¢.

Equipment at the side of this cabin includes metal traps.

Mountain men liked to use a rifle called a Hawken, which required metal balls, little patches, and gunpowder. The patches held the ball on top of the gunpowder. Modern rifles use bullets that combine gunpowder and a metal ball in one piece.

A man in nineteenth century costume fires a flintlock rifle in a field at the Western National Buckskin Rendezvous.

Mountain men also carried large knives, whetstones to sharpen them, and tomahawks. A knife and tomahawk were good for protection. A mountain man also used his knife to skin beavers and cut meat.

One of a mountain man's most important supplies was a liquid musk called castor, an oily, brown, smelly substance taken from the glands of dead beavers. Mountain men put the musk near their traps to attract beavers.

Another important item was the mountain man's "possible sack." It was made from buckskin, or the hide of the bison, often called the buffalo. The sack contained scissors, tobacco, pipes, and extra deerskin for mending clothes. Some mountain men also carried lucky coins or other good luck charms.

It may have been easy to mistake mountain men for Native Americans. Both wore long hair, sometimes braided.

Mountain men copied the way some Native Americans dressed. They wore buckskin pants and shirts, and their clothes had fringes. Mountain men also wore buffalo-hide moccasins. Mountain men waded in cold creeks, streams, and rivers to set traps. Leather boots and wool socks would never have lasted as long as buffalo-hide moccasins. Buffalo hide treated with smoke did not shrink.

Mountain men needed hats to keep their heads dry and warm. Hats also served as a way for mountain men to recognize each other. Some had wolves' tails hanging from their hats. Many mountain men wore raccoon skin or leather hats. Some sewed beads and porcupine quills on them.

Mountain men ate a lot of meat, and seldom ate vegetables or fruit. If they had no food with them, they killed birds or animals. One of their favorite foods was buffalo. They liked the buffalo hump the best. They also liked raw buffalo liver and bone marrow.

Mountain men wore distinctive hats, which helped them to recognize each other.

Fur trappers arrive at the annual rendezvous near Scotts Bluff, Nebraska. Traders met here with buyers from the East, exchanging furs for goods. Native Americans also took part.

HIGH JINKS AND TRADING

Fur trading companies built trading posts that were sometimes called forts. Native Americans and mountain men took their beaver pelts to sell at the posts.

Posts could be dangerous places. Some Native Americans did not like them. They feared that the posts would eventually bring more white people to the area. Some tribes attacked the posts.

Grand Portage National Monument, a restored fur trading post in northern Minnesota.

Posts were expensive to run. Companies had to ship supplies to the trading posts, and had to pay people to live in them. The Rocky Mountain Trading Company had a post called Fort Henry. A Native American tribe raided the boats that brought in supplies. Another tribe attacked the company's trappers. The company finally decided not to use trading posts anymore. They wanted to get beaver pelts in a safer and cheaper way.

The company abandoned Fort Henry and began sending their trappers out into the wilderness. They told the trappers where to bring the beaver pelts, usually in late spring. Making plans to meet at a certain time and place is called a "rendezvous," a French word that means an appointment or date. The company's rendezvous idea changed the fur trade.

The rendezvous was an important business and social event for mountain men, who usually lived far from the cities. Sometimes they went without seeing another person for months. At a rendezvous a mountain man relaxed and traded his year's supply of pelts for supplies.

The first day of a rendezvous was a day for "high jinks," or fun. Mountain men ate as much food as they could. Most of them talked to anybody who would listen. Many of them had not talked to another human being for a year. A lot of the talk was about trapping beavers, fighting Native Americans, and bravery.

Actors ride horses while dressed in the kinds of raccoon-skin hats and buckskin clothing worn by mountain men.

Mountain men also held contests during a rendezvous. They raced their horses or mules and had shooting matches. Sometimes they wrestled each other. They also had eating contests. The mountain men had contests for almost everything.

The fur companies knew the mountain men needed to get supplies at the rendezvous, since they had lived on the frontier all year. They wanted tobacco, sugar, tea, and coffee. They needed gunpowder, rifle balls, and traps. Blankets, mirrors, and cooking utensils were also necessary. The mountain men gave "hairy bank notes," or beaver pelts, to pay for their supplies. A beaver pelt was worth between four and nine dollars. Most trappers came to the rendezvous with several hundred pelts.

The companies wanted the pelts that the mountain men had, and they had the supplies that the mountain men needed to go back trapping. So the companies set the prices for supplies, and the prices were high. Tobacco, coffee, and sugar cost 10¢ a pound in St. Louis, and $2 a pound at a rendezvous.

A rendezvous usually lasted about two weeks. Then the mountain men went back to the frontier, usually with enough supplies to last another year. Meanwhile, the beaver pelts went east on the fur companies' wagons.

The rendezvous way of trading lasted less than 20 years. The last rendezvous was held in 1840.

JOHN COLTER

In 1804, Meriwether Lewis and William Clark explored the land from St. Louis, Missouri, to the Pacific Ocean. The Lewis and Clark Expedition, also called the Corps of Discovery, lasted two years.

In August 1806, the Corps of Discovery was on its way back to St. Louis. The group met Joseph Dickson and Forrest Hancock, who were going westward. They were trappers who had traveled before on other fur-trapping journeys. In spite of Native American attacks, bad weather, and accidents, they wanted to trap again.

John Colter was a member of the Corps of Discovery. He was fearless, strong, and able to take care of himself in the wild. He also enjoyed adventure. He had spent two years in the wilderness and knew there were many beavers in the West. Lewis and Clark allowed Colter to leave the expedition in order to travel with the trappers and become a mountain man.

In 1807, Manuel Lisa put together a group of 50 trappers and traders. Lisa's group went west on the Missouri River. They used a riverboat without sails called a keelboat. Where the Platte and Missouri Rivers join, they met John Colter. Colter was again heading east to go back to St. Louis. Lisa asked Colter to work for him as a guide and trapper. Colter agreed and once again went west.

Lisa's men built a protected trading post, which he named Fort Raymond after his son. The post was also called

There are hot springs and geysers at Yellowstone National Park.

Fort Lisa and Fort Manuel. The post was located where the Yellowstone and Bighorn Rivers meet. Lisa sent John Colter and the other trappers from the post, instructing them to tell Native Americans in the area that he would trade rifles, knives, and blankets for beaver pelts. He also wanted the trappers to find beavers.

While away from the post, Colter found what is now called Yellowstone National Park. Colter told others of the area's geysers, boiling mud pots, and hot springs. Many never believed him.

Later, some members of the Blackfoot tribe captured Colter. Instead of killing him, they decided to hunt him like they hunted animals. Colter's clothes were taken from him, and he was told to run for his life. He ran more than five miles (eight km) to a river. He jumped in the cold water and hid under some driftwood. That night he sneaked away.

Colter had no shoes or clothes, and only roots and berries to eat. Colter walked for seven days until he finally reached the safety of Fort Raymond. A few weeks later he left the post to explore and trap.

After almost 10 years in the West, Colter went back to St. Louis. He never returned to beaver country.

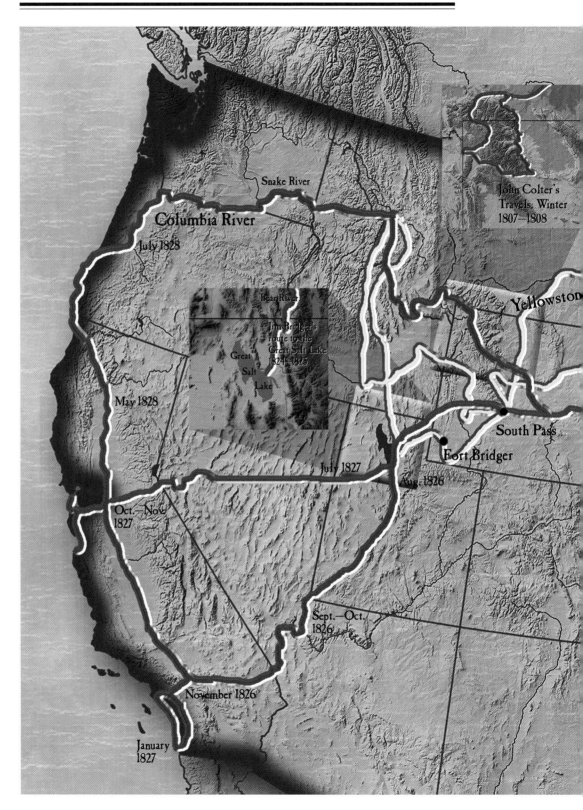

Snake River

Columbia River

July 1828

John Colter's
Travels, Winter
1807–1808

Bear River

Jim Bridger's
route to the
Great Salt Lake
1824–1825

Yellowston

Great
Salt
Lake

May 1828

South Pass

Fort Bridger

July 1827

Aug. 1826

Oct.–Nov.
1827

Sept.–Oct.
1826

November 1826

January
1827

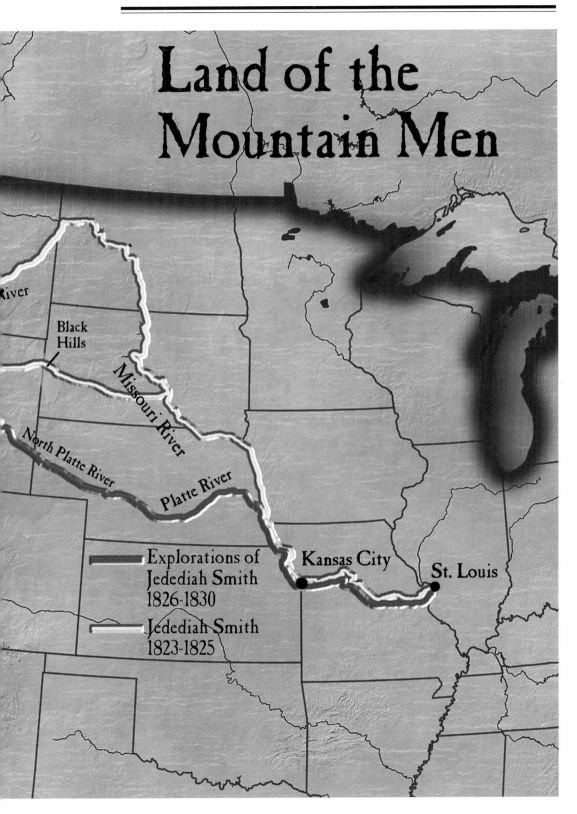

Land of the Mountain Men

River

Black
Hills

Missouri River

North Platte River

Platte River

Explorations of
Jedediah Smith
1826-1830

Jedediah Smith
1823-1825

Kansas City

St. Louis

JEDEDIAH SMITH

Jedediah Strong Smith was one of the best mountain men. He was also a well-read explorer. Smith was born in Bainbridge, New York. His family moved from New York to Erie, Pennsylvania. Smith learned how to hunt and fish in Pennsylvania's forests. Later, the Smith family moved to Ashtabula, Ohio.

When Smith was young he received a book from a family friend about the expedition of Lewis and Clark. Their travels excited Smith. He wanted to experience western adventures, too. Finally, he left Ohio and went west.

In St. Louis, Missouri, Smith joined William H. Ashley's group of trappers. Smith soon found out that he was not like other trappers. Smith liked to read the Bible. Most of the others did not like to read. Smith had read some of the works of great writers. Most of the other trappers knew little of such works. Smith also listened more than he talked. Other trappers enjoyed telling farfetched stories about themselves. In 1822, Ashley and his group of trappers went up the Missouri River in keelboats.

In 1823, Smith was involved in a conflict with the Arikara Native Americans. Ashley's trappers had landed on the shore of the river to trade with the Arikara. The Arikara attacked and the trappers scrambled to get back to their boats. Ashley sent a man to Fort Atkinson to get help and Colonel Henry Leavenworth came to assist. Colonel Leavenworth and the Arikara signed a peace treaty.

A grizzly bear attacked Jedediah Smith in the Black Hills of present-day South Dakota and Wyoming.

The trappers divided into two groups and headed west. Smith's group went through the Black Hills, a small mountain range in the present-day states of South Dakota and Wyoming. In the mountains, a grizzly bear attacked Smith. The other trappers hit the grizzly, but it kept mauling him. The bear clenched Smith's head in its jaws and shook him, then it dropped Smith and left.

Smith suffered several broken ribs in the attack. One ear hung from his head. He also had several other bad head wounds. One of the other trappers used an ordinary needle and thread to reattach Smith's ear. He also sewed Smith's other wounds. After several days, Smith was healthy enough to travel again. He and his group continued west.

A man dressed as a trapper carries a rifle across his shoulder for the Green River Rendezvous, an annual celebration in Pinedale, Wyoming, to honor mountain men and trappers who settled the West.

Smith and his group reached a treeless valley. They traveled into the valley and came to the Big Sandy River, which Smith noticed was flowing west. Smith knew that they had crossed the continental divide, since water flows to the west on the western side of the divide, and to the east on the eastern side. Smith knew they had to be across the Rocky Mountains.

The place where Smith and the trappers crossed the Rocky Mountains is called South Pass. South Pass is in present-day western Wyoming. Other men had crossed the Rocky Mountains through South Pass. But Smith was the first to go through the pass from east to west.

In the following years, Smith explored the areas that would become California and southern Oregon. In 1831, he and a group headed south toward present-day New Mexico. Smith was riding ahead of the group looking for water. A Comanche Native American war party found Smith and killed him. He was only 32 years old.

Badlands are located near South Pass on the Oregon Trail, in the Wind River Mountain Range of Wyoming.

JIM BRIDGER

Jedediah Strong Smith was one of the best mountain men, but Jim Bridger was probably the most famous. Bridger had many abilities, each necessary to being a good mountain man. He was an expert shot and had an excellent memory. Army General Grenville M. Dodge once remarked that Jim Bridger had a map of the entire West in his mind. Colonel E.Z.C. Judson, who wrote under the name Ned Buntline, wrote stories about Jim Bridger called Bridger Stories. These stories made Bridger famous throughout the country.

In the winter of 1824-1825, Bridger and some other trappers were camping along the Bear River in present-day Utah. The men wondered where the river went. Bridger followed the river and found that it emptied into a big lake with salty-tasting water. Jim Bridger was the first non-Native American to see the Great Salt Lake.

In August of 1830, Bridger and four of his friends bought the Rocky Mountain Trading Company. They renamed their new company the Rocky Mountain Fur Company.

A few years passed, and Bridger knew there were less and less beavers to trap. He left trapping and opened a trading post on the Green River along the Oregon Trail. His trading post, named Fort Bridger, included a store, cabins, a blacksmith shop, and corrals for horses, oxen, and mules. It was the only trading post within hundreds of miles on that

Jim Bridger (1804-1881), famed scout, mountain man, and explorer.

section of the Oregon Trail, and the first to serve not only trappers and Native Americans, but also settlers moving west.

Jim Bridger kept his trading post for many years. Once in a while, he went back to the mountains and lived as a mountain man. He eventually retired to his home near Kansas City, Missouri, and lived to be an old man.

An actor dressed in 1800s clothing demonstrates the activities of a trapper during a living history program at Fort Bridger, Wyoming. He is preparing an animal skin to be stretched over a fire.

In 1842, Jim Bridger built Fort Bridger in southwestern Wyoming. The fort became a stopping point for emigrants traveling the Oregon and Mormon Trails.

SILK MAKES BETTER HATS

In 1820, beaver pelts were valuable. Mountain men received between four and nine dollars per pelt. Less than 20 years later, they received one dollar per pelt. The pelts were no longer in demand.

Mountain men were excellent trappers. They trapped hundreds of thousands of beavers, and eventually created a beaver shortage. Usually, when something is hard to find it becomes more valuable. However, this was not true for beavers. There were fewer beavers, but their pelts were worth less money. Worms were the biggest reason beaver pelts were less valuable. These were not fishing worms— they were silkworms from China. The worms produced silk that could be made into beautiful fabric.

People stopped wanting hats that were made of beaver pelts. Instead they wanted hats made of silk. Beavers were no longer in demand, and the mountain men that hunted them were no longer needed.

While hunting for beavers, mountain men explored the West for America. They found trails to cross the western plains. They found passes to cross the western mountains. Most importantly, they discovered that the West was a place where American settlers could live. The mountain men changed American history.

INTERNET SITES

http://www.whiteoak.org/index.html

The White Oak Society is a non-profit organization providing "living history" interpretations of the fur trade era within the Great Lakes region. Explore the Learning Online Centre and visit with a voyageur or an English gentleman. Learn about beaver hats and birchbark canoes. Also includes a library with book reviews and links to other sites.

http://www.worldweb.com/ParksCanada-Rocky/history.html

This Web site, maintained by the Rocky Mountain House National Historic Site, provides a good history of the fur trade in Canada. Includes sections on history, beaver hats, early trading posts, and Native Americans.

These sites are subject to change. Go to your favorite search engine and type in "mountain men" or "fur trappers" for more sites.

History buffs: educate readers around the country by passing on information you've learned about mountain men. Share your little-known facts and interesting stories. We want to hear from you!

To get posted on the ABDO Publishing Company Web site, email us at "History@abdopub.com"

Visit the ABDO Publishing Company Web site at:
www.abdopub.com

GLOSSARY

Arikara: A Native American tribe that lived in villages.

Black Hills: A small mountain range in South Dakota and Wyoming.

Buckskin: An animal skin, usually deer or cow, that has been tanned or treated so that it can be comfortably worn.

Continental divide: An area of high ground on a continent. River systems on each side of this high ground flow in opposite directions.

Hairy bank notes: A name mountain men used for beaver pelts.

Independents: Trappers who did not work for any one particular fur company.

Keelboat: A riverboat with a keel but without sails. They were often used for carrying freight.

Lewis and Clark Expedition: From 1804 to 1806 Meriwether Lewis and William Clark led an expedition to explore the territory gained in the Louisiana Purchase. The expedition's name was the Corps of Discovery.

Loner: A person who enjoys being alone, who does not need the company of other people.

30

Marrow: The material inside a bone.

Musk: A liquid that mountain men used to lure beavers to traps.

Oregon Trail: A 2,000-mile (3,219-km) trail from Independence, Missouri, to the Willamette Valley, Oregon.

Pack animals: Generally horses, mules, or dogs used to carry supplies or people.

Possible sack: A buffalo or buckskin sack that mountain men used to carry scissors, tobacco, pipes, extra deerskin, and perhaps a lucky coin.

Predator: An animal that kills other animals for food.

Rendezvous: A French word people use to name a meeting at a certain place and time.

Rocky Mountain Trading Company: A fur trading company begun by General William H. Ashley and Andrew Henry.

A North American beaver.

INDEX